Our Lady of Guadalupe
And Her Dear Juanito

By Marlyn Evangelina Monge, FSP

Illustrated by Amy Rodriguez

Pauline
BOOKS & MEDIA
Boston

Library of Congress Control Number: 2022933694

CIP data is available.

ISBN 0-8198-5475-1

ISBN 978-0-8198-5475-9

Cover art by Amy Rodriguez

All rights reserved. No part of this book may be reproduced or transmitted in any form or by any means, electronic or mechanical, including photocopying, recording, or by any information storage and retrieval system, without permission in writing from the publisher.

"P" and PAULINE are registered trademarks of the Daughters of St. Paul.

Copyright ©2022, Daughters of St. Paul

Published by Pauline Books & Media, 50 Saint Pauls Avenue, Boston, MA. 02130-3491

www.pauline.org

Printed in Korea

OLOFAHDJ SIPSKOGUNKYO5-2087 5475-1

Pauline Books & Media is the publishing house of the Daughters of St. Paul, an international congregation of women religious serving the Church with the communications media.

2 3 4 5 6 7 8 9   30 29 28 27 26

Dedicated to my beloved mom, Evangelina Monge:
By her daily lived example she has passed on to me,
my siblings, and her grandchildren
a deep faith in God and loving devotion to Our Lady.
Thank you for teaching us how to be authentic disciples of Christ.

Dark. Still. Quiet.

Those are the words that best described the pre-dawn morning as Juan Diego found the well-worn path at the foot of Tepeyac hill. In many ways this December Saturday morning was like any other day: the world around him was asleep. His footsteps were the only sound that broke the silence.

Suddenly the most amazing sound filled the sky. The music was like singing birds. It was so beautiful he stopped to enjoy it. *Where is it coming from?* he wondered. *It seems to be coming from the top of this hill. It is like nothing I have ever heard. Am I dreaming? Am I in heaven?*

Just as suddenly as it started, the music stopped. Everything was quiet once again. Then a gentle voice called out in his native language, Nahuatl, "Juanito, Juan Dieguito."

He recognized the affectionate nickname, but wondered who was calling him. *I have never seen anyone else on this path at this hour.* The voice, like the music, came from the summit. He climbed quickly to the top of the hill just as the sun began to rise. There he saw a young indigenous woman standing. The ground and plants near her gleamed like emeralds and turquoise. Her clothes glowed and it appeared that rays of sunlight were coming from her. Then she looked at him and smiled. *She is the most beautiful lady I have ever seen!* he realized.

"Come closer, my son," she beckoned with a nod of her head.

She must be a princess, Juan Diego thought, so he knelt before her. Speechless in her presence, he just listened.

Looking at him with love, she asked, "My most beloved son, Juan Diego, where are you going?"

He replied, "I am going to the church in Tlatelolco for Mass and to learn more about the faith."

"My dearest son," she said, "I am the ever-Virgin Mary, Mother of the true God. I want a church built on this site so I can be a faithful Mother to you and all the people of this land. It will be a place where I can lead all my children to God. A place where people can come to seek my help. I am a compassionate Mother to all who cry out for mercy, to all who entrust their worries and fears to me, and to people of different ancestries. I am your Mother."

"Go to Mexico City, my son," she continued. "Let the bishop know that I have sent you. Tell him everything you have seen and all that I have told you. Go in peace and do the best you can."

Juan Diego responded, "I am your humble servant, my most noble Lady." He left immediately and took the path headed west to Mexico City.

When, at long last, he was given entrance into the bishop's home, Juan Diego told Bishop Juan de Zumarraga everything he had heard and seen. But the bishop didn't believe him. He thought that Juan Diego had imagined it all, or worse that it was the work of a demon. Disappointed, Juan Diego returned the way he had come.

Walking and lost in thought, he came across the place where the Virgin Mary had appeared to him—and there she was again!

"My most beloved Queen, I did what you asked," Juan Diego explained sadly. "I told him everything, but the bishop did not believe me." He took a deep breath and continued, "I beg you, My Lady, please send a more noble person, someone the bishop will believe. I am just a poor man, and this business is too grand for me."

Mary replied, "Listen carefully, my son. I have many servants whom I could send. They would do whatever I asked. But I have chosen *you* for my mission.

You are the right person. Return tomorrow, my son. Tell the bishop that it is I, the Virgin Mary, Mother of the true God, who sends you and wants a church built on this site."

"For you I will gladly go," Juan Diego responded. "Tomorrow afternoon, when the sun is about to set, I will return here with the bishop's answer."

The next morning, Sunday, December 10, Juan Diego went to Mass. Then he returned to the bishop.

When he was allowed to see the bishop, Juan Diego explained all that had happened since he had left the bishop the day before.

"Our Lady asks that you build a church in her honor on Tepeyac so that she can be a mother to our people," he reminded the bishop.

Throughout Juan Diego's story the bishop asked many questions and Juan Diego answered them all. *Maybe what this man says is true*, the bishop thought. *I need to be sure it is Our Lady he has seen.*

The bishop said, "Go and tell your lady that I would like a sign to prove that she is the Mother of God."

Juan Diego was so happy walking back to Tepeyac! He could hardly wait to see Mary and tell her what the bishop said this time.

At long last Juan Diego arrived at the hill where the Blessed Mother waited for him. "My Lady," he started, "the bishop wants a sign to prove that you are Mary most holy and that it is your wish for a church to be built here."

"Thank you, my dearest child, for doing as I asked. You are a most faithful servant." Mary smiled at him as she spoke. "Come back tomorrow. I will give you the sign to take to the bishop so that he will believe."

After telling her that he would return, Juan Diego went home.

The next day, Juan Diego arose and prepared to go to Tepeyac. But before he could leave, he received word that his uncle, Juan Bernardino, was seriously ill and had a terrible fever.

I know my Lady is waiting for me, but my uncle has been like a father to me. I must go to him at once, Juan Diego reasoned.

He spent the whole day caring for his uncle and looking for a healer who could give him some herbal remedies to cure his uncle. "Nephew," Juan Bernardino called weakly. "I am worse. I fear I will not live much longer. Please go to Tlatelolco in the morning and ask a priest to come quickly."

The next day—Tuesday, December 12—before the sun rose, Juan Diego set out for the church. There were two paths he could take. *If I take my normal route, I will go up to the top of Tepeyac and then my Lady will stop me to ask why I did not go yesterday*, he thought. *My uncle is dying; I cannot be delayed even by my most beloved Mother. I will have to take the longer route and go around Tepeyac. Then once I bring back the priest I will return and explain everything to her.* Having made up his mind, Juan Diego took the path that circled the hill's base.

As he turned around a bend in the road, Mary was there surrounded by a white cloud. "Where are you going, my son?" she asked.

Juan Diego knelt before her. "How are you this morning, my most beloved Lady? Are you well?" He kept his face down, not wanting to meet her eyes. "Please do not be angry with me for not coming yesterday. My uncle is dying. I am rushing to ask a priest to hear my uncle's confession and to anoint him. After I have done that, I will come back and do whatever you wish. Please forgive me. I will return tomorrow without fail."

 The Blessed Mother looked at him with great tenderness. She said, "My dearest son, do not worry about this illness. Am I not here, I who am your Mother? Are you not beneath my shadow and my protection? Are you not under my mantle and cradled in my arms? Do you need something more?" After a moment she continued, "Do not worry about your uncle's illness. He will not die from it; indeed, he is already healed."

Juan Diego was amazed at all he heard, and he did not doubt Mary. Relieved he said, "Give me the sign you wish to send the bishop. I will set off at once."

She replied, "My beloved and sweet son, go to the top of the hill where you saw me before. Cut the flowers you find there and gather them in your tilma. Then bring them to me and I will tell you what to do and say."

Without another word, Juan Diego hurried toward the summit. *How can there be flowers this time of year?* he wondered as he climbed. *It is so cold and this land is rocky. No flowers can be growing here.*

Reaching the top, Juan Diego gasped at the sight. *I have never seen such beautiful flowers anywhere. They are all in full bloom!* Where only the day before there were cacti and rocks, now roses of every color covered the hilltop.

Juan Diego quickly cut the sweet-smelling blossoms, turned his tilma around to collect them, and returned to the Blessed Mother.

She took the fragrant flowers and arranged them. Placing them once again in his cloak, she said, "Here is the sign that you are to take to the Bishop. My most beloved and faithful son, do not unfold your tilma except when you are with the bishop. With this sign he will believe and build the church."

When she finished speaking, Juan Diego took the road to Mexico City. As he walked as quickly as possible, he was very careful not to let a single flower fall. The sun was up by the time he reached the bishop's residence.

After waiting a long time, Juan Diego was allowed to see the bishop. Bowing before him, Juan Diego said, "Mary most holy asks again that you build a church on Tepeyac. She sends you the sign you asked for." With that, Juan Diego unfolded his tilma so that the flowers fell at the bishop's feet.

"*Madre Santísima*, Mary, most holy!" the bishop exclaimed, sinking to his knees.

Juan Diego realized that the bishop was not admiring the array of beautiful roses. Instead the bishop was staring at the tilma. Juan Diego looked

down and was surprised to see an image of the Virgin Mary on his tilma. It looked just like the Lady he had seen on Tepeyac.

"Where did you get this cape and these flowers?" the bishop asked.

"The tilma is mine, and it is the same one I wore the other two times I came here. This morning my Lady sent me to the top of Tepeyac to gather these flowers. I was surprised to find them. She arranged them in my tilma. As for how her image came to be here, I do not know."

"It is a miracle and a sure sign that it is Mary the Mother of God whom you have seen and spoken with," declared the bishop.

Full of joy at accomplishing his mission for our Lady, Juan Diego went to visit his uncle, Juan Bernardino.

"Hello, Juan Diego," greeted Juan Bernardino.

"My uncle, you are looking much better," Juan Diego remarked.

"Thanks to a beautiful woman who came to me, I am now well," explained Juan Bernardino. "Not long after you left to get the priest, she appeared in my room. She said that she wished a church to be built where you had seen her. She also said that she wanted to be known as Holy Virgin Mary of Guadalupe." After speaking some more, they realized that Our Lady of Guadalupe had appeared to Juan Bernardino at the same time she had told Juan Diego that his uncle was healed.

As neighbors came to talk to Juan Bernardino about his miraculous recovery, Juan Diego stepped to a quiet spot under a tree.

Bowing his head, he made the sign of the cross and prayed. "My dearest Lady, thank you so much for asking God to heal my uncle. I promise that for the rest of my life I will tell everyone that you are our mother and that we can turn to you with all our needs."

Author's Note

From December 9-12, 1531, Our Lady of Guadalupe had appeared five times—four times to Juan Diego and once to Juan Bernardino. She had spoken to the two indigenous men in the language they understood best, Nahuatl.

Immediately after her image was revealed on Juan Diego's tilma, it was taken to the bishop's private chapel and then to a nearby church where many people venerated the image and asked for her intercession.

On December 26, 1531, the image of Our Lady was taken in procession to the quickly-built chapel on Tepeyac. Juan Diego—Our Lady of Guadalupe's faithful and humble servant—spent the rest of his life living in a hut near Our Lady's little church. There he welcomed all pilgrims. He told them about Our Lady of Guadalupe's love for them and encouraged them to get to know her and her son, Jesus. Juan Diego Cuauhtlatoatzin, which means "talking eagle," died in 1548. He is the first Roman Catholic indigenous saint of the Americas. His feast day is on December 9, the date that Mary first appeared to him. The feast of Our Lady of Guadalupe is celebrated on the day her image appeared on Juan Diego's tilma—December 12. It is customary to celebrate the Feast of Our Lady of Guadalupe by serenading Mary early in the morning with songs commonly referred to as *las mañanitas*.

Before long, the chapel was too small for all the people who traveled to bring to Mary their needs and concerns. Over the centuries bigger churches were built on Tepeyac to accommodate the crowds. Today the Basilica of Our Lady of Guadalupe and the tilma bearing her image have over 12 million visitors a year. Countless people have experienced miracles after praying for Our Lady's intercession.

Symbolism in the Image of Our Lady of Guadalupe

Our Lady's image on the tilma is full of symbolism. The symbols would have been particularly meaningful for the indigenous people of Mexico. Here is a small list and explanation of just some of them:

1. **Face and hair**: Our Lady of Guadalupe has the complexion of the indigenous people of Mexico. Specifically she is a *mestizo*, a combination of Mexican and Spanish peoples. This symbolizes that she is for all people. Her eyes are downcast. She knows that she is not a god. She is humble, full of tenderness and compassion. Her loose hair signifies that she is a virgin.

2. **Hands and body**: The indigenous people prayed not only with their hands but with their whole bodies. Mary's hands show her to be in a pose of prayer. Her left knee is slightly bent, which could have been understood that she was in movement, as if she was caught in mid-prayer dance. Since Our Lady of Guadalupe is shown praying, this also tells us that she is not a god.

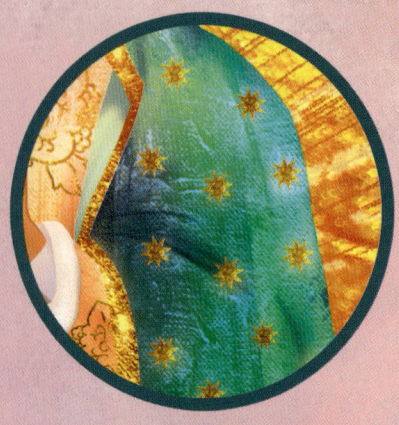

3. **Mantle**: The color of Mary's mantle would have told the native population that she was royalty, since only their native emperors wore turquoise cloaks. In addition it is covered in stars, which points to her coming from heaven.

4. **Sash**: Our Lady has a black ribbon above her waist. This means that she is expecting a child and may even give birth soon.

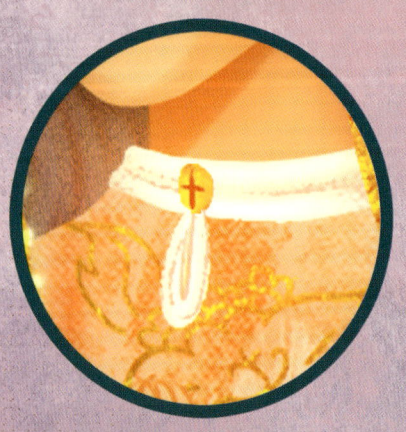

5. **Brooch**: Aztec art usually depicted their gods and goddesses wearing a jade oval brooch. Mary's brooch, however, has a cross on it. The indigenous people who saw the tilma would have understood immediately the combination of the Aztec and Christian cultures—they would have properly interpreted that Mary is noble but not a goddess. Furthermore, the cross instantly tells us that she belongs to the God of Christianity.

6. **Four-petaled flower**: For Aztecs this flower was used to depict the presence of their greatest deity. This flower is on Mary's tunic at one place—directly over her womb. It, therefore, tells us that the baby she carries is God. She is the Mother of God.

Words to Know

indigenous: refers to people who are native to a place—like the Aztecs in Mexico.

Nahuatl [NAH-wa-tl]: the language spoken by Juan Diego, Juan Bernardino, and Our Lady of Guadalupe.

Tepeyac [teh-pay-YAK]: the name of a hill located in what is now Mexico City. It was here that Our Lady appeared to Juan Diego.

tilma: a simple cloak-like outer garment worn by indigenous men of Mexico. It could be worn as a cloak across the shoulders or in front like an apron.

Tlatelolco [Tla-te-LOLE-co]: the town near where Juan Diego lived. He traveled there often to go to Mass at Saint James the Greater church and to receive catechesis. Tlatelolco was a little more than three miles (five kilometers) away from Tepeyac.

Prayer to Our Lady of Guadalupe

Our Lady of Guadalupe, your message to Saint Juan Diego is a message we all need to hear—you are our Mother and we can go to you with all our needs, no matter what language we speak or what color our skin is. You are the mother of all people who love your Son, Jesus. You are my heavenly mother. Pray for our world, Mary, that we may see each other as brothers and sisters and work toward the coming of your Son's kingdom. Amen.

Prayer to Juan Diego

Saint Juan Diego, sometimes I feel small and unimportant. You showed me by your life that I do not need to be big and important to be Mary's child and do God's will. Like you, I want to be faithful and humble. Like you, I want to do whatever God asks of me. Please pray for me, that I may recognize and follow the ways that God wants me to take. Amen.

About the Author

Sr. Marlyn Evangelina Monge has been a Daughter of St. Paul since 2005, and she currently serves the people of the Bay area through our Pauline Book & Media Center in Menlo Park, California, and through outreach evangelization. Before entering the convent, she taught bilingual kindergarten for six years, taught in her parish's religious education program, and volunteered with the youth ministry program. Sister Marlyn has a master's degree in education and enjoys finding ways to help children discover the wealth of their faith through the stories she writes. She is the author of ten books with Pauline Books & Media, with *Our Lady of Guadalupe and Her Dear Juanito* being the latest. Sister Marlyn is a proud tía (aunt) to her six nieces and nephews who live in New England.

About the Illustrator

Amy Rodriguez is a digital artist and children's book illustrator based in sunny Los Angeles, California. She attended Loyola Marymount University where she graduated from the School of Film and Television with a B.A. in animation. Amy creates bold, colorful illustrations and seeks to share the joy and beauty of the Catholic faith through her art. She is the illustrator of various Catholic children's books that can be found on her website: www.amyrodriguezart.com This is her first book with Pauline Books & Media.

Thank You!

When you read this book and share it with others, you help us in the work we do as Daughters of St. Paul. This book is part of our mission to communicate God's love.

We are praying for you!

Connect with us or send us prayer intentions at pauline.org.

Pauline
BOOKS & MEDIA